Benefits of Lucid Dreaming

Be in control of your dreams and your life

Termina

Copyright © 2017 by Termina

All rights reserved. No part of this book may be reproduced, scanned, or distributed in any printed or electronic form without permission.

This book is designed to provide information and inspiration to readers. It is sold with the understanding that the author is not engaged to render any type of psychological, legal, or any other kind of professional advice. The content of each article is the sole expression and opinion of its author. No warranties or guarantees are expressed or implied by the author's choice to include any of the content in this volume. The author shall have no liability or responsibility to any person or entity regarding physical, psychological, emotional, financial, commercial damages, special, incidental, or consequential by the information contained in this book.

Contents

Foreword

Chapter 1:

Why Explore This

- What is a dream?
- Why are Dreams Exaggerated?
- What is Lucid Dreaming?
- The Basics
- Thoughts from Dream Realms
- No two dreams are ever the same

Chapter 2:

Remembering and Journaling

- Develop the Power to Dream
- Recall
- Maintaining a dream journal:
-

Chapter 3:

Common Questions

Chapter 4:

What Is It Like

- The Experience

Foreword

Fantastic, bizarre, and even inconceivable things regularly occur in dreams, however, most people do not realise that there are explanations for their dreaming, nor do they realise that they can be in control of the results.

Occasionally, dreamers can realise the explanations for the occurrences playing out in their dreams; and some as a final result understand the term lucid dreaming. They are empowered by the knowledge that the domain they are experiencing is a production of their own imagination, and these lucid dreamers may consciously determine the final result of their dreams. They create and metamorphose objects, individuals, situations, worlds, and even themselves. By the measures of the familiar world of physical and social reality, they can do the inconceivable.

The domain of lucid dreams supplies a more immense stage, greater experiences, than average life for almost anything conceivable, from the frivolous to the sublime. You may, if you chose, enjoy an unworldly festival, zoom to the stars, or visit mystical lands. You may join those who are trying out lucid dreaming as a tool for problem resolution, self-healing, and personal maturation. Or you may research the implications of teachings from ancient customs and accounts from modern psychologists that indicate that lucid dreams may help you discover your deepest identity-who you truly are.

Chapter 1:
Why Explore This

What is a dream?

An event transpiring in a world belonging to the mind when the objective senses, waking mind, has withdrawn to rest. This is where the subjective mind, the spiritual, the essence of a person can develop conditions that enables the waking person to shape their actions by guidance or warnings, to aid in making life a perfect existence.

Why are Dreams Exaggerated?

The will and conditioned beliefs are suspended during sleep, therefore the dream mind is more open and adaptable to excitability and possibilities than the waking mind.

What is Lucid Dreaming?

A dream where the dreamer is aware of dreaming. During lucid dreaming, the dreamer can exert little to full control over the dream characters, narrative, and environment. These dreams can be more than escapist fantasy, they are an alternate reality.

In the Following pages we will discover how to wake up in your dreams.

Do the Advantages justify the time and effort demanded for mastering lucid dreaming?

The Basics

Undeniably, life is short and we spend approximately one-third of our lives sleeping. Many of us are in the habit of sleepwalking through our dreams, unaware that we at any time can control our dreams. We rest senselessly, through many, many chances when we could be totally cognizant and alive. More importantly we have the ability to expand on our experiences, experiences that can aid us in our waking life.

Is sleeping through dreams our best practice to use in our restricted lifetime?

Not only are you missing out on your finite stock of time to be alive, but you're neglecting adventures and lessons that may enrich the rest of your lifetime. By waking up to your dreams, you'll add to your experience of living and if you use these added hours of clarity to experiment and exercise your brain, you are able to likewise better your enjoyment of your waking hours.

Benefits of Lucid Dreaming

Dreams are a source of knowledge and experience; all the same they're frequently neglected as a vehicle for researching reality. In the dream state our bodies are at ease, yet we see and hear, propel about, and are still able to learn. When we make great use of the dream state, it's almost as though our lives were doubled: rather than a ninety years, we live hundreds.

We may carry not only knowledge but likewise moods from the lucid dream state to the awake state. When we wake up laughing with joy from a fantastic lucid dream, our wakening mood is lightened with feelings of delight.

This transfer of positive feeling into the waking state is a crucial facet of lucid dreaming. Dreams recollected or not, often colour our mood upon waking up, occasionally for a great part of a day. Even as the negative after effect of "bad" dreams may cause you to feel as though you got up on the wrong side of the bed, the favourable feelings of a pleasant dream can give you an emotional pick up, aiding you in the beginning the day with self-assurance and energy. This is more genuine with inspirational lucid dreams.

Thoughts from Dream Realms

We, the human being, are a world composed of infinitesimal atoms, also known as matter, connected to a greater circle or parent world, the Universe. Dreams are symbols of subjectivity to guide the objective (the waking mind or material mind). Subjectivity is the spiritual part of a person. The soul is that circle of the individual person that exists outside the physical world. All thoughts and desires first enter the soul or material mind and then cast themselves on the spirit. Commonly, the soul becomes so filled with material or present ideas, that the spiritual symbols are veiled in a crowded mind.

If we tap into more matter of the greater circle, we catch more material to increase our physical human circle to objective or subjective growth: if we absorb spiritual or mind matter from the body of creative source, we can enlarge and uncrowd our own lives to the assimilation of the matter we received from the parent world.

To obtain spiritual or material matter is essential for higher self growth. To feed on the material diet of our physical existence (waking hours) alone, contracts and distorts our experiences in our waking hours.

An objective life, the exterior life of man, is one of the smallest compounds in real life. Dream life is fuller of meaning and teaching of the inner, or Divine Self life. The mind is developed by exercise just as the muscles of the body. The more these are cultivated by drawing from the parent world, the more knowledge or power our minds take on.

The mind receives education from communing with the dream in the great circle. Consult with your whole nature, your Divine for a fuller life experience.

No two dreams are ever the same
Whatever symbol appears to the dreamer is the one which is required in the 'now'. No two persons can ever have the same symbology. Peoples dream perception wavers, much as it does in waking hours.

Everything as Einstein stated is Energy, and because energy is constantly in perpetual transmutation, no two energies can ever be alike. Nothing has a precise identical twin. Not even human identical twins, there is always something unique from one to the other to be found; and this unique variety runs through all creation.

It may seem that you have identical dreams, but there is always some variation. It is important to take note of this for interpretation of your dream.

Chapter 2:
Remembering and Journaling

It's been stated that "everything is dependent on remembering", and this is surely realistic of lucid dreaming.

Develop the Power to Dream

Lucid dreaming happens when your mind is awake while your body is still asleep. However, unconscious sleep and dreams are critical to your cognitive and emotional health so it's important to **get** enough rest. A well-rested conscious mind is much more likely to become awake and alert inside a dream. Go to bed early.

Keep the mind clear and as free from material (waking mind) rubbish as possible. We can relax our mind and body to the receptive mood required for dreams to appear as realities by practicing meditation, breathing techniques or doing something that you as an individual finds restful prior to sleep.

By applying the practice to heighten your consciousness in dreams and once you've had the experience of recognizing that you're dreaming and that your possibilities are far better than you had thought, you are able to imagine what a similar realization may be like in your waking life, apply this and create an improved waking life.

Recall

Finding out how to remember your dreams is essential if you wish to practice dream lucidly. Until you have dream recall, you will not attain the benefits of lucid dreams. There are two reasons for this.

First: without remembering, even if you accomplish having a lucid dream, you won't recall it. We all have lost many lucid dreams among the many thousands of dreams we have blanked out in the normal flow of our lives.

Second: great dream recall is essential to become lucid (easy to understand) you have to realize that your dream is a dream, while it's occurring. Since these are your dreams that you are trying to recognise, you have to get acquainted with what they are like.

You understand what a dream is, generally. However dream stories are not always simple to differentiate from accounts of events that really occurred. Dreams generally look like life, with particular noted exceptions.

These exceptions are trespasses of your expectations about the behaviour of the world. So, you have to get to understand what your dreams are like, and particularly, what is dreamlike about them. You are able to achieve this by accumulating your dreams and examining them for dreamlike factors.

Before you practice lucid dream induction techniques, you must be able to remember at least one dream nightly. The following tips will help you accomplish this goal.

The opening move to great dream recall is getting adequate sleep. If you're rested, you'll discover it easier to centre on your goal of remembering dreams, and you won't mind taking the time during the night to note them. A different reason to sleep longer is that dream periods become longer and closer together as the night continues. The first dream of the night is the quickest; approximately ten minutes in length. After eight hours of rest, dream flows may be from forty five to sixty minutes long.

Benefits of Lucid Dreaming

It is not uncommon to have have more than one dream during a rapid eye movement, REM (dream period) each are short stimulations that are most frequently forgotten. It's broadly accepted among sleep experts that dreams are not remembered unless the sleeper wakes up directly from the dream, instead of after advancing to additional stages of sleep.

If you sleep too deeply to wake up from your dreams, set an alarm to arouse you at a time when you are likely to be dreaming. As rapid eye movement periods happen at roughly ninety-minute intervals, great times will be multiples of ninety minutes from your bedtime. Target the later REM points by setting the alarm clock to go off at four and a one-half, six, or seven and a one-half hours after you go to sleep.

An important requirement to recalling dreams is motivation. For most of us we only need to set an intention to recall dreams and remind ourselves of this intention just prior to bed. In addition, it might help to tell yourself you'll have intriguing, meaningful dreams. Placing a dream journal by your bed and noting your dreams as soon as you wake up will help fortify your resolve. As you note more dreams, you'll recall more. Hints for maintaining a dream journal are presented below.

Get into the habit of inquiring the moment you wake up: "What was I dreaming?"

Do this immediately upon waking or you may blank out some or your entire dream, due to distractions from extra thoughts. Don't move from the position you wake up, as body motion may make your dream more difficult to recall. Likewise, don't consider the day ahead, this too may delete your dream recall. If you recall nothing, keep attempting for several moments, without moving or considering anything else.

Commonly, pieces and shards of the dream will present to you. If you still cannot recall any dream, ask yourself:

"What was I just imagining?" and "How was I precisely feeling?"

Analysing your thoughts and senses frequently may provide the essential clues to let you recall the whole dream.

Take notice of any clues as to what you may have been feeling, and attempt to reconstruct a story from them. When you remember a scene, ask yourself what occurred prior to that, and prior to that, re-experiencing the dream in reverse. It does not take long to form enough skill at this to activate a detailed replay of a whole dream simply by centering your attention on a shard of memory.

If you are unable to remember anything, attempt envisaging a dream you may have had and note your current feelings, list your present fears to yourself, and inquire,
"Was that a dream?"
If after a couple of moments all you recall is a mood, write the details in your journal. Even if you cannot recall anything in bed, issues or scenes of the day might remind you of something you dreamed the night prior. Be prepared to observe this when it occurs, and note whatever you recall.

In evolving dream recall, as with any other skill, advancement is occasionally slow. Don't be disheartened if you don't succeed initially. Everybody improves with practice. As soon as you remember your dreams, at least once nightly, you are ready to attempt lucid dreaming. This will not take long to accomplish at this stage of preparation. And a substantial percentage of individuals who get this far will already be having lucid dreams.

Maintaining a dream journal:
Acquire a notebook or diary for recording your dreams. Ensure the notebook is pleasant to you and entirely dedicated for the

aim of noting dreams. Put it by your bedside to remind yourself of your aim to put down dreams. Note your dreams directly after you wake up from them. You can either record the whole dream upon waking from it or put down short notes to elaborate later. You do not have to be a gifted author. Your dream diary is a tool, and you're the only one who's going to study it.

Do not wait until you get up in the morning to make notations on your dreams. If you do, even if the particulars of a dream appeared exceptionally clear when you woke up in the night, by break of day often people forget the details.

We appear to have inbuilt dream erasers in our brains which make dream experiences harder to remember than waking ones. So, ensure you record at least some key words about the dream directly upon waking up from it.

When recording, Identify the way images and characters appear and sound and smell, and include the way you felt in the dream- emotional responses are crucial clues in dreamland.

Note anything strange, the sorts of things that would never happen in waking life: flying animals, or the power to breathe submerged, or puzzling symbols. Sketch specific pictures in your journal, even if they are rough sketches.

The drawing, like the piece of writing, doesn't have to be art. It's simply a way for you to arrive at an intuitive and memorable association with a picture that may help you achieve lucidity in succeeding dreams.

Place the date at the top of the page. Note your dream below the date, carrying forward for as many pages as needed. If you recall only a shard of a dream, note it, regardless how insignificant it may look at the time.

And if you remember a whole dream, title your journal submission with a little, catchy title that catches the issue or mood of the dream.

Once you start to amass some raw material in your dream diary, you can review your dreams and inquire about them.

Reading over your journal will help you become acquainted with what is dreamlike about your dreams so you'll be able to recognize them while they're still occurring -and become lucid.

Chapter 3:
Common Questions

Fears regarding lucid dreaming:
Can lucid dreaming be life-threatening for some?

The majority of lucid dreams are favourable, bringing rewarding things, much more so than average dreams. However, there may be a few individuals who find the experience of lucid dreaming unpleasant and, in a few cases, highly disturbing. For this reason we do not advocate lucid dreaming for everybody.

On the other hand, we're convinced that for individuals no more than "typically neurotic", lucid dreaming is altogether harmless. Different individuals will utilize lucid dreaming for different aims; it makes little sense to admonish the typical adventurer of the dream world away from lucid dreaming as some may utilize it in a less than optimal fashion. If, after studying this book, you've serious reservations regarding lucid dreaming, then we advocate that you do not continue. Just make certain that it's really yourself to which you're being true. Do not let others impose their personal concerns on you.

I'm afraid that if I learn to cause lucid dreams, all my dreams will turn lucid. Then what?

The philosopher P. D. Ouspensky underwent conflicting emotions concerning *"half-dream states"* as he named lucid dreams: *"The beginning sensation they raised was one of amazement. I expected to discover one thing and discovered another. The following was a feeling of extraordinary delight which the „half-dream states, and the possibility of encountering and understanding things in quite a fresh way, gave me. And the 3rd was a particular fear of them, as I very soon discovered that if I let them take their own course they'd start to grow and expand and infringe both on sleep and on the waking state."*

Once you start entertaining this distressful line of thinking, likely you'll quit having lucid dreams. Without your consent there's truly very little chance that all dreams would become lucid. Lucid dreaming takes effort. Lucid dreams happen only rarely unless you go to sleep with the calculated and definite aim to become conscious, or lucid, in your dreams. Therefore, you'll be able to regulate (and restrict, if essential) the frequency of lucid dreams.

I believe that dreams are messages from the unconscious, I'm afraid that consciously commanding my dreams would interfere with this crucial procedure and strip me of the Advantages of dream interpretation.

Dreams are not letters from the unconscious, but things produced through the interactions of the unconscious mind and conscious mind. In dreams, more unconscious knowledge is useable for our conscious experience. But, the dream is not at all the exclusive domain of the unconscious. If it were, individuals would never recall their dreams, as we don't have waking access to what isn't conscious.

The individual, or dream ego, that we feel being in the dream is the same as our waking awareness. It perpetually influences the events of the dream through its anticipations and biases, even as it does in waking life.

As for the Advantages of dream interpretation, lucid dreams may be examined as productively as non-lucid ones. Indeed, lucid dreamers occasionally interpret their dreams while they're occurring. Becoming lucid is likely to alter what would have otherwise occurred, but the dream may still be interpreted.

Benefits of Lucid Dreaming

Occasionally in lucid dreams I find situations of spirituality, accompanied by feelings of the presence of power or energy. At these times my awareness expands much beyond anything I've felt in waking life, so that the experience appears much more real than the truth I know, and I get frightened. I can't continue these dreams for fear that I'll never wake up from them, as the experience appears so far out of the domain of waking existence. What would happen if I was not able to wake myself from these lucid dreams? Would I die or go crazy?

This fear you relay amounts to little more than concern of the unknown. There's no evidence that anything you accomplish in a dream may affect your basic brain physiology in a sense that's adverse. And, as vivid as a dream might be, it cannot last any longer as the raw course of REM periods-at most 60 minutes approximately. Naturally, as explorations of the world of dreams have truly just started, there are bound to be areas as yet unmapped. But you shouldn't fear pioneering them. The feel of intense anxiousness that attaches to the sudden onset of unusual experiences in dreams is an innate part of the orientation reaction: it's adaptive in the waking world for an animal in a new situation or dominion to look 1st for peril. However, the fear isn't necessarily relevant to what is occurring. You need not dread physical harm in your dreams. When you detect yourself in the middle of a fresh experience, release your fear and simply see what occurs.

They state that if you die in your dream, you truly will die. Is this real?

If it were real, how would anyone know? There's direct evidence to the contrary: a lot of individuals have died in their dreams without any ill effects, according to the accounts they gave after waking up- alive. Furthermore, dreams of death may become dreams of rebirth if you permit them.

I'm afraid that I might not have what it takes to cause lucid dreams. What if, after doing all of the drills and devoting much time to it, I still can"t learn to cause lucid dreams? If I place all that time into it, and do not acquire any results, I'll feel like a failure.

Among the biggest stumbling blocks in learning almost any skill is trying too hard. This is particularly the case with lucid dreaming, which demands that you sleep well and have a balanced frame of mind. If you discover you're losing sleep while scrambling to have lucid dreams without result, release your efforts awhile. Relax and forget about lucid dreaming for a couple of days or a couple of weeks. Occasionally you'll discover that after you relinquish, lucid dreams will come out.

I'm presently undergoing psychotherapy. Is it all right for me to attempt lucid dreaming? Can it assist in my therapy?

If you're in psychotherapy and wish to try out lucid dreaming, talk it over with your therapist. Not every therapist will be informed about lucid dreaming and its significances for therapy, so make certain your therapist realizes what you're talking about and is acquainted with the current data. Lucid dreaming might be instrumental in psychotherapy. If your therapist does not believe that lucid dreaming would be a great idea for you at this time, abide by his or her advice. If you take issue, you can either trust the judgment of your present therapist on this matter or find a different therapist, ideally one who recognizes how to help you to work with your lucid dreams therapeutically.

Chapter 4:
What Is It Like

If you haven't as yet experienced a lucid dream, you might find it hard to imagine what it's like. Although you have to feel it to truly know what it's like, it's possible to acquire an idea of the feel by comparing lucid dreaming to a presumably more familiar state of awareness: the one you're in this minute! The following experiential exercise will direct you through a tour of your daily waking state of consciousness.

Spend approximately one minute on every step.

The Experience

Look

Become aware of what you witness: note the wide-ranging and brilliant impressions- shapes, colours, motion, dimensionality, the whole visible existence.

Hear

Become mindful of what you hear: record the various sounds accepted by your ears-a diverse range of strengths, pitches, and tonal calibres, maybe including the old-hat miracle of speech or the marvel of music.

Sense

Become mindful of what you contact: texture (unwrinkled, rough, dry, pasty, or wet), weight (gravid, light, solid, or void), joy, pain, hotness and cold, and the remainder.

Likewise observe how your body feels right now and equate that to the many additional ways it feels at additional times, played out or industrious, stiff or limber, dreadful or pleasant, and so forth.

Sense of taste

Become aware of what it is like to taste: taste a number of individual foods and substances, or recall and vividly conceive their tastes.

Sense of smell

Become mindful of scents: the smell of warm bodies, land, incense, smoke, fragrance, java, onions, alcohol, and the ocean. Recall and imagine as many of them as you are able to.

Taking a breath

Notice your breathing. A minute ago you likely were not consciously aware of your breathing even though you have unconscious competently breathed in and out fifty times while doing this drill.

Hold your breath for a couple of moments. Let it out. Now take in a rich breath. Note that being conscious of your breathing lets you alter it by choice.

Emotions

Become mindful of your feelings. Recall the difference between rage and joyfulness, tranquillity and fervour, and as many other emotions as you care to experience. How real do emotions feel?

Opinions

Pay attention to your opinions. What have you been imagining while doing this drill? What are you imagining right now? How real do opinions appear?

"I"

Become mindful of the fact that your domain always includes you. You're not what you witness, hear, recall, or feel; you have these experiences.

Benefits of Lucid Dreaming

Fundamentally, you are who is aware. You're always at the center of your multi-dimensional existence of experience, but you're not always consciously mindful of yourself.

Briefly repeat the practices with the accompanying difference: At the same time you handle each of the assorted aspects of your experience, be mindful that it is you who's observing these things ("I see the...").

Knowingness of knowingness
Lastly, become knowledgeable of your awareness. Awareness centres on objects external of ourselves, but it may itself be an object of awareness.

In the light of physical experience, we appear to be distinct and have limited centres of awareness, each solely from our inner worlds. In the light of infinity, mystics tell us, we're ultimately all one-the limitless awareness that's the source of being. Here, experience can't be adequately conveyed by language or meditation.

Wrapping Up
Think about how baffled most of us are when attempting to comprehend the origin and purpose of our lives, and equate this

baffled frame of mind to that of the non-lucid dreamer attempting to rationalize the events of the dream in the wrong terms. Our dreamlands make much more sense and provide many more possibilities when we recognize we're dreaming. Therefore, a way which makes clearer the nature of the things in our waking lives would lead to expanded understanding of the context of our lives, and better access to our expansive potential and creativeness.

Lucid dreaming is not a consummate path to enlightenment. However, lucid dreaming aids in taking us to our goals and are a signpost pointing to the higher consciousness, a reminder that there's more to life than individuals are commonly aware of, and an inspiration to seek a guide who recognizes the way.

About the Author

Termina listed as a global Self-Help expert and Author also known as 'The Happy Magnet' has the uncanny ability to tilt the odds so the best will happen resides with her family in Australia and believes in navigating the changing world of experiences.

As an Expansion Mentor and with a corporate background in personal development, design and business, Termina holds a range of qualifications including Transformational Leadership, Public Speaking and Medicine. Also an exponent of Feng Shui, Termina uses her knowledge of Energy and Quantum physics to support individuals and organizations by increasing their success in financial situations, relationships, health or inspiration. Termina loves to use her imagination and has gained the title 'Master of Imagination', she has used her skills to work on many residential and commercial projects, including an open design radio station, Fox Studios and a variety of set designs, where her own artwork was exhibited for TV and film.

Termina holds the knowledge of communication in high acclaim in particular non-verbal language as this has been an exceptional skill in moving her towards her chosen goals. Termina has worked with many great minds including Bob Proctor and Peggy McColl; and adds that seeking knowledge, self-improvement and possibilities through mentors and books is the greatest gift to ourselves.

Termina also believes imagination is the source of advantage, and everybody has the good fortune of this ability, and her book, Festival of the Imagination, is one of her many non-fiction titles which explores this all-important subject.

Festival of the Imagination is one of many non-fiction books by Termina. Termina calls herself a student of self-actualization. It was through her studies and introspection practices that she was able to tap into her unique soul signature and states that she is guided by source. *"At all times we carry with us all the answers. There is nothing in the physical world that will truly give us the ultimate answer; our unique soul print and purpose in life; and it is because of this only ourself has the true answers for what makes us happy or why we are here. We only require external tools, or mentors to get us started and guide us in a direction towards connecting with our soul's voice. With the right tools and mentors, we are on our way to unleashing our true, powerful self."*

Termina credits communication and self-actualization practices for her success and harmony in her life. Another one she credits is Feng Shui as a guide to alignment for choices. *"It was through my studies and practice of Feng shui that I discovered the importance this ancient art plays in our life. 33% of our experiences are created through our physical visualization board, our environment. When we apply the principles of Feng Shui our lives become the choices we desire, we are in control of our own experiences at all times and good fortune is attainable. Through Feng Shui I have seen improvements and successes in my own life along with the many others who have appointed my services."*

For more information about this author
And other books:
www.terminaashton.com
www.terminafengshui.com
www.perpelflame.com
www.thehappymagnet.com

www.ingramcontent.com/pod-product-compliance
Lightning Source LLC
Chambersburg PA
CBHW050450010526
44118CB00013B/1768